The Passage of the Years

by

Hugh Barnes-Yallowley

Front cover painting 'Firle Place' (View from Pleasure Ground) 2001
by Nicolas Gage,
8th Viscount Gage.

(I acknowledge the valuable information in the Firle Church Guide by the Rev FBR Browne and Canon James Woodward. The church guide was revised by Jen White and Liz Hill in 2013. H B-Y)

ISBN 9781979006002

Published by Hugh Barnes-Yallowley

St. Richard's Prayer

Thanks be to Thee
my Lord Jesus Christ,
For all the benefits which
Thou hast given me,
For all the pains and insults
which Thou hast borne for me,
O most merciful Redeemer,
Friend and Brother.
May I know Thee more clearly,
Love Thee more dearly,
And follow Thee more nearly.

St Richard (1197-1253) is the Patron Saint of Sussex

Foreword

Hugh has been a friend of mine for over 40 years and in fact he also knew my father the 6th Viscount Gage.

Although compared to my own family, which has been at Firle Place for the last 500 years, Hugh is a comparative newcomer, but for the last 55 years, he has taken an exceptionally keen interest in all aspects of village life and its history.

I am therefore very pleased and honoured to be associated with this short book which gives a brief outline of my own family's strong and ancient bond with the village as well as several other aspects of Firle and the surrounding region which are often overlooked by modern historians.

Hugh is the author of two books and this volume 'The Passage of the Years' is dedicated to Firle and the surrounding influences of Charleston as well as several other local individuals, including the artist Eric Ravilious whom Hugh and I both agree deserves far more international recognition than he has enjoyed to date.

Hugh has been inspired (as we all have) by the beauty of the surrounding countryside which so greatly influenced Ravilious as he drew, etched and painted many of the houses still existing in and around Firle as well as important landmarks within the area.

From little facts about our church to more personal descriptions of village life, I am sure that you will enjoy this little volume as much as I did.

Viscount Gage

Author's Foreword

I have had a connection with Firle for many years and was very happy when my wife Anne and I secured Gibraltar Farm in 1970 and we finally became a *real* part of the village.....In fact, I do believe that in the many years that we have been in the village, between us, we have managed to be members of every committee, every initiative and change that has taken place in the village in the last half-century!

All the places described in this book are all very well known to me as are most of the people. It would not be an exaggeration to say that most of the characters described were, and many still are, very good friends of mine.

For instance, Peggy Angus is a very important part of Firle's immediate past history as she allowed and encouraged the artist Eric Ravilious to develop and produce those stunning watercolours of the Sussex Downs...but my memories of her are much more personal.

Not only did Peggy teach my eldest son Jonathan to paint but Anne and I still recall summer evening picnics with Peggy and her very close friends, the Kennedys on the Downs above Peggy's house, 'Furlongs'.

Those and many other Firle memories are so precious - as are the memories triggered by all the places described in this book.

I sincerely hope that you enjoy sharing them with me.

Hugh Barnes-Yallowley

A Downland Sanctuary

Out of the swirling galaxies of gases moving but immovable in the mists of time I am part of immortality the spark of the infinite an all seeing eye of the all seen and I yearn to know those who live, albeit temporarily, outside this constant space in the confines of time itself.

The energy that is the creator that is beauty, truth and strength combined knows all, sees all, understands all but with infinite gentleness and compassion hopes for the redemption of all those locked outside of immortality.

I must go for you and see for myself, I must dive as a hawk seeing both the great expanse and yet picking out the tiniest shrew running between the standing corn.

I will focus from that realm which needs no focus down into time itself and see how those enslaved by its moving hands have understood anything of that immortality which is to be simply laboured for that hour which exists.

Hurtling through that impossible barrier which is time itself on which is rent only by what mortals call death, my hurtling vision focused on a thousand years which are as nothing but I saw in them a Downland Sanctuary and from it came yearnings of immortality over all the hours and days of those thousand years.

Praise was given to the Creator, who is forever, favoured beseeched, promises made, and confessions unburdened.

Surely in that brief span and in the still brief lives that are the seconds of the minutes and the minutes that are all the years of the hour that are the century's I saw joy and happiness, all that is good and beautiful and I saw sadness for of that is in mortality made and not the infinite love of the infinite truth that is of all time.

I am a traveller in time and I see a sanctuary that strives to be beyond time and the sanctuary is a people and within people and it is here as I see the hidden green waves on the Sussex Downs.

The Setting

Since time immemorial Sussex has been a green and pleasant land in which to dwell.

Mount Caburn is a softly rounded downland spur and bathed in the brightness of the early morning sun or set against the richly red cloud bank of the evening one can sense a time warped quality; its thin ridged crown, the outline of the well preserved Iron Age ditch surrounding an encampment constructed some 500 years before Christ.

From the security of this hill fort, our forebears gazed across the dark forested land in the Glynde Valley towards Black Cap with its many sacred burial chambers of some 3000 years ago. Between these ancient Downs secure in their shaded valley lies Firle, its name derived from the old English for an oak covered land of Fierol.

In the village a strong downland spring - never known to have failed - of pure water finds its way down into the Glynde tributary which is also fed by many other streams, including one from Stamford Brook, marked by the base of a stone cross. Out of the darkness of the Wealden Forest and into the mudflats of Glynde Reach the tributary flows down into the Ouse, the estuary whose bands stretched from Southease to Tarring Neville and which served to promote Lewes as a settlement and port. When the Norman conquerors landed at Pevensey, they found the Sussex downlands already extensively colonised.

Many centuries later this turning point in our history is brought to mind by the tomb of the wife of one of Williams's trusted followers at Lewes where her name Gundera, is also a reminder that the invaders from Normandy were of Scandinavian ancestry with fair skin and blue eyes.

Curiously this link with northern France has been maintained. Many years later the Huguenots sought refuge here and stone quarried in Normandy was used in a number of Sussex buildings some five centuries after the conquest.

The Gage Family

There are many constants in the village of Firle, but by far the most enduring and important is the presence of the Gage family.

They have been the custodians of Firle Place and Firle Estates for over 500 years and it is no exaggeration to say that the Gage family is the glue that binds together this part of Sussex.

The first Gage to establish himself in Firle, was Sir John Gage, who was counsellor to Henry VIII and whose son, Sir Edward was created High Sheriff of Sussex by Mary Tudor. He was made famous or should we say infamous for overseeing the burning of the Lewes Martyrs - an event which has never been forgotten and is commemorated to this day.

At the time, the Gage family was unambiguous about its Roman Catholic faith and as a result there were difficult times for nigh on 250 years until the 7th baronet Sir William Gage renounced his Catholic faith.

Immediately, the family was able to rebuild and improve Firle Place, and in 1720, Sir William's cousin Thomas Gage was created the 1st Viscount Gage.

The unbroken line continues to this day and Firle Place remains the home of the 8th Viscount and his family who all understand both the history and the easy informality of the people of Firle and the importance of Firle Place as an iconic cultural and architectural gem, rather appropriately nestling within the understated but sumptuous splendour of the South Downs.

The Village

The village houses and cottages are relatively unaltered since they were built some centuries ago and still retain the calm and rural quality of bygone days, although most of the craftsmen, which once inhabited this village - cobbler, tailor, blacksmith, miller, butcher and a baker have gone and only one beer house remains out of the original five.

This is the Ram Inn, named after the crest on the coat of arms of Lord Gage and built in the 1800s. A major part of the building is still intact and some of its unique local atmosphere is preserved. It faces up the village street, where a variety of periods of Sussex buildings can be seen.

Close by the Victorian schoolhouse of 1845, lie Polecat Cottages of the 17th century, also previously a beer house. Facing The Crescent is the Black House, one of the few independent houses in the village which, like some on Lewes High Street, was hung with polished mathematical tiles. The style was adopted to improve the facade of timber framed houses to simulate brickwork and give them a more dignified Georgian appearance.

Next door is Little Talland, once the home of the novelist Virginia Woolf, whose London origins gave her group the name of the Bloomsbury Set. They, like so many others, found inspiration in the atmosphere of the South Downs as writers, painters, poets and freethinkers. They included Virginia's sister, Vanessa Bell and her children, Julian, Quentin and Angelica; the painter, Duncan Grant and the writer, David Garnet. Into an extraordinary and colourful household at Charleston Farmhouse in the Parish of Firle there gravitated other young intellectuals, budding economist Maynard Keynes, TS Eliot, Lytton Strachey, Roger Fry and EM Forster.

Clive Bell and Duncan Grant lived on at Charleston and to their respective deaths. Duncan Grant was buried next to Vanessa Bell in Firle churchyard.

Next to Little Talland, but in more recent times, lived one of our most distinguished professors of early English music, Robert Donnington.

In the same way that Charleston Farmhouse will forever be associated with the Bloomsbury set, there is one other property within the Gage firmament, which has been made famous by an artist who has not acquired the Bloomsbury set notoriety, but nevertheless deserves a far more prominent place both in Firle's as well as in art history - and that is Eric Ravilious.

His most famous painting is 'Tea at Furlongs'. It is a deceptively simple painting (shown below) and yet it symbolises so much about Firle and the Sussex countryside.

The picture is of a simple, frugal but very English afternoon tea whose backdrop is a late summer/early autumn view of the countryside. The only slightly discordant note is the parasol which has the depressing look of an adapted rickety gentleman's black umbrella , but more likely, as 'Tea at Furlongs' was painted in August 1939, the dark parasol is hinting at the blackness already spreading through Europe....and the Sussex sky depicted in the painting would not be as clear for many years to come.

Tea at Furlongs - Eric Ravilious 1939

In fact, Ravilious is primarily known for his work as a war artist but it would appear that his technique was formed here in Firle.

He said of Furlongs - a simple flint and brick cottage - *'Furlongs altered my whole outlook and way of painting, I think because the colour of the landscape was so lovely and the design so beautifully obvious.'*

Ravilious took that simplicity with him and it continued to be reflected in all of his subsequent work.

'Furlongs' did not belong to Ravilious - he was a guest of Peggy Angus who he had met when they were students at the Royal College of Art.

Peggy had acquired the cottage after a little bit of a struggle, but in spite of its idyllic situation, life there was very spartan and occasionally very hard. For instance, a primitive stove provided both heating and cooking facilities and there was no running water or electricity. The rustic proletarian simplicity of the cottage is clearly illustrated in another of Ravilious' paintings entitled 'Interior at Furlongs'.

Ravilious was definitely a Sussex man and in spite of being extremely well travelled and eventually settling in Essex, he would always return to his roots. His family had moved to Eastbourne when he was very young and in fact he studied at the Eastbourne School of Art where eventually he returned to teach and that is where he met his wife - another artist -Tirza Garwood.

Ravilious' painting style is very distinctive and has an almost naive childlike quality but he was also a very accomplished wood engraver and his engraving style is reminiscent of the work of Paul Nash, who influenced many inter-war artists, including Tirza.

Paul Nash, who taught at the Royal College of Art, was not only a great influence on a number of Sussex artists, but he was also very much part of the Bloomsbury group , which itself had a connection with the artists centred on Peggy Angus' home, Furlongs.

One unusual aspect which the Charleston and Furlongs groups shared and which bound them together, was their over-fondness for intra-marital, extra- marital and many other shades and flavours of personal relationship, for which the Bloomsbury group gained a certain much-deserved notoriety.

Although not in the same league as the Charleston inhabitants, one can safely say that the Furlongs group also enjoyed their friendships and relationships to the fullest extent.

Some of Eric Ravilious' best-known and celebrated paintings were the watercolours completed in Firle. His set of greenhouse-themed watercolours were painted within the market garden on the Firle Estate.

It would seem that Ravilious' work is gradually coming more and more into fashion and this was best illustrated by a 2017 exhibition at the Towner gallery in Eastbourne. The exhibition included not only his work, but that of his Sussex-based contemporaries . It was designed to give the viewer some context and included work by several other artists who had been taught or influenced by Paul Nash.

In spite of its limited size, 'Furlongs' became every bit as artistic and creative as Charleston Farmhouse.....as Peggy Angus and Ravilious were joined by other intellectually fertile people such as Percy Horton who lived at Firle Tower and was Ruskin Professor of Drawing at Oxford University.

'Furlongs' soon developed into a nucleus of creativity and intellectual pursuit from painting to the singing of Elizabethan rounds.

Between the village shop, which still today sells a little of everything in the traditional manner, and the Woolpack Cottages, formerly a public house, lies the Dock.

This small side road contains the main village spring of fresh water rising from the Downs, which flows into a small waterway and eventually reaches the fishponds. Known as 'The Stews' these were once the mediaeval fish larder for the Manor of Heighton St Clere on the hill above what is now Firle Park and which gives its name to Heighton Street.

The water from the fishponds after running water through watercress ponds eventually forms a small lake, the home of Canada geese, mallard, herons and swans.

There are still traces of freshwater clams, which date from Roman times in the lake. Surplus water runs off under the main road and across into Glynde Reach which, although recently dammed (1976) was originally tidal and flows into the Ouse.

It was this route which was used in the 18th century to bring stone which had been shipped over from Caen in northern France to Firle for the rebuilding of the Tudor Firle Place, which was then redesigned and rebuilt with a distinctly French manorial flavour mixed with early Georgian in which it is seen today.

Near Heighton Street the remains of the Manor house are now only soft undulations in the fields above the Stews. The home farm is still there and Quentin and Olivia Bell live in what was originally a Dower House of Firle Place and which is remarkable for the mediaeval king post at the front of the stairs which probably came from the Manor of Heighton St Clere.

Heighton Street joins the Old Coach Road which skirts the hem of the Downs and is part of Firle. It leads towards the cottage of Beanstalk, once a beer house, from the woods surrounding the wall of Firle Park with the golden walk in a plantation of beech, oaks, and sycamore and the silver walk in a plantation of aspens and silver birch. Along the Old Coach Road and to the south is the gamekeepers lodge built as a tower or folly, designed in all probability mainly to view the Firle Estate, it nevertheless provided the gamekeeper with an excellent opportunity to sight the London train when Lord Gage was returning from the House of Lords to the railway station built at Glynde in 1846.

As the signal went up at Glynde the gamekeeper could raise a flag on the tower, which could be seen from Firle Place to enable the coach to start from Firle in time to pick up his Lordship - the fourth Viscount Gage (1807 to 1877).

His great-grandson, the sixth Viscount Gage, greatly loved Firle - from the days when he and his new bride were drawn up Firle Place drive in a haywain pulled by the village men to the days in his old age when he listened to the carollers who had walked with their swinging candle lanterns up that same drive to sing to his family and guests, the Firle Carol dedicated to him.

Christmas is dawning
Like the first morning
Children are singing
Like the first day.
Let me too praise him
He who is coming
Each new renewing
Upon our way.

God is descended
Into each person
Born in all people
As he first came.
Open your ears then
Like mother Mary
To Angels singing
Glory God's name.

Open your eyes then

As did the sages
To God's great riches
Given for men.
Then let your lips sing
As did the shepherds
Telling of God's peace
Sent now and then.

Thus may we echo
God's new beginning
Offered to all men
Each glad new day.
Death, life and rebirth
His re- creation
Sing down the ages
Truth is for aye.

And in thanking them he would say, *'I am happy that we, like generations before us, are here to turn our hearts to the Christmas story and follow the tradition of my family and this ancient house.'*

At the centre of Firle, in the friendly graveyard on a substantial mound standing above and yet at the heart of the village, is Firle church, the sanctuary of prayer and Christian worship from earliest Saxon days and it was from those times that St Richard's Prayer originated. Indeed, it is more than likely that a small Druid sanctuary stood on this site and later a Roman one.

There are the remains of a Roman villa at Beddingham, and Firle church and the villa lie on the route which early man would have taken when passing along the Downs via the Long Man at Wilmington.

Also looking up to Firle church is Firle Place which has been the home of the Gage families for six centuries. This remarkable house provides the beautiful setting for its celebrated collection of paintings of English and European Masters, fine furniture and superb porcelain.

The relation between the house and the church is close.

Gage ancestors are buried in the crypt and in the churchyard and there is a remarkable collection of monuments, early brasses dating from 1563 to 1595 and an alabaster effigy of Sir John Gage and his wife Philippa by Garat Johnson. This splendid work in marble and brass records the history of the clothes of the time and the setting has recently been greatly enhanced by the magnificent John Piper window in memory of the sixth Viscount Gage with its slate inscription carved by John Skelton

The Firle Resistance

Although the idea of a village-based resistance movement may suggest shades of Dad's Army, Britain's secret Army was Winston Churchill's idea as a result of known German plans for the invasion of Britain.

Needless to say, if there was an invasion, the South Coast would be very much on the front line. So in 1940 a secret corps of civilians was trained in readiness. The brave men were trained in Guerilla techniques and you may be surprised to hear that Firle had its very own resistance cell, with a fully equipped underground bunker.

Obviously, the participants were sworn to secrecy and they all managed to keep the secret for over 50 years! In fact, it wasn't until 1996 that a book entitled *'The Secret Sussex Resistance'* by Stewart Angel was published.

In total there were 26 so-called 'Auxiliary Unit Underground Hideouts' throughout East Sussex, including one in both Rodmell and Firle.

The smallest of all was the Firle patrol and it had four members. Bill Webber, a local gardener was patrol leader. Under his command were Tom Smith, Jack Cornwall and

John Pilbeam. Jack and John were employed by the Firle Estate.

The hideout was situated south of the village in a wood known as the Firle Plantation and was built by the Royal Engineers. It consisted of a wooden structure with the later addition of an Anderson shelter and it contained three bunks and a galvanised water tank.

The Firle volunteers were all involved in night training with other groups and in 1943, all units were asked to volunteer to be parachuted into France as part of a pre-invasion plan. Both Bill Webber and Tom Smith from the Firle patrol participated in the parachute training.

Thankfully, as it became clear that there was little likelihood of the German invasion, all the patrols continued the operation, although the training was no longer as intense, until they were finally asked to stand down towards the end of 1944.

Although these men were not called upon to fight on our behalf, we have to admire not only their courage, but their ability to maintain secrecy for so many years, especially in such a tightly knit village, such as Firle.

We salute them.

Firle Bonfire Society

The current Viscount Gage is President of the Firle Bonfire Society and it would be unforgivable if a book about Firle did not at least mention this very important aspect of village life.

The Society has a long history with written records from as far back as 1878, although one suspects that The Bonfire Boys have been around for much longer!

There has always been opposition to Bonfire Societies and Firle is no exception although it is interesting to note that the Gage family have always been great supporters and to this day, it is Viscount Gage who lights the fire on Bonfire Night.

Bonfire Night celebrations have become something the village looks forward to every year and it was only in the 1970s when Firle Bonfire Society sadly folded because of a lack of support.

In the late 70s, Finn Kennedy, Hugh Barnes-Yallowley with their families and guests built a bonfire in the park and let off fireworks. This rekindled an interest in Firle Bonfire Night.

Finally, in 1981, a meeting was called to resurrect the Bonfire Society and since that inauspicious start, the Society has gone from strength to strength and is now firmly re-established as a major local event.

The Church

The downland sanctuary of St Peter's has a richly varied and interesting history.

Before the Norman Conquest, Firle belonged to the Abbey Wilton. After the conquest King William gave Firle to his half-brother Robert, Earl of Morton and his son then gave it to the Abbey of Grestain in Normandy which already had a Priory of Wilmington and it is for this reason that in the very early days the church was called Grissens Minster.

Somewhere between 1179 and 1204 Abbot Robert of Grestain gave Firle church to the Dean and Chapter of Chichester.

The oldest part of the present church is the north door which is a Norman one dating from 1100 and may have been placed in that position at a later date because it has scratched on the outside two Mass Dials which are small sundials with a hole in the centre for the Gnomon to cast a shadow.

The majority of the rest of the church tower, nave and chancel were built in the early 1200s, and have been very little altered since that time.

The remainder of the church is largely of the 1300s, including particularly the Piscina in the chancel and the altar window of the South Chapel with its original glass angels and quatrefoils of the 14th century and the south door which has crosses cut in it by pilgrims at that period. The Gage chapel was added in the 16th century.

There has always been a very close relationship between the Gage family and Firle church. Gage ancestors are buried in the crypt and in the churchyard and there are early brasses, monuments and effigies commemorating the Gage family in the Gage chapel.

Here is a little more detail about our church:

The Font. The Mary and Martha window. As you enter St Peter's, the Font on your left symbolises our entry into life and into the church through baptism. To the left of the Font, you will see a charming stained-glass window in the style of William Morris, depicting St Martha and St Mary, installed in 1885. In 2013, it was decided to move the Font closer to the Mary and Martha window and during this reordering of the church, three 17th-century graves were discovered. Two of them are dedicated: One to Martha, wife of John Swaffield, a Vicar of Firle. Martha died aged 28, in 1681. The other is dedicated to John Harrison, who *'dyed the 19 daye of October 1643 aged 19 yeares five monethes and fowerdays'.* The third grave is without dedication.

The Tower. The tower at the far end of the church is 13th century and in the 1700s housed five bells. These eventually deteriorated and were replaced in 2004, thanks to valiant efforts in fundraising.

We now have four new bells, cast at Whitechapel near London Bridge using material from the old bells. An additional two bells were obtained from a Roman Catholic Church in Brighton, by chance, also dedicated to St Peter. Our bells are currently electronically chimed, but could be converted to be manually chimed. The dedication of the six bells and details of their weight, tone etc are listed on a board in the tower. You can see the wooden frames, now restored, which originally held the bells.

The Kempe Window. On the left, just before the door to the Vestry, you will see a very special stained-glass window depicting an angel with shepherds with the inscription *'On earth peace, goodwill toward men'*. If you look closely at the left-hand border of the window, you will see a wheatsheaf, the identifying icon of Charles Eamer Kempe, born in 1837, in Ovingdean. Kempe has been described as *'more notable than William Morris or Edward Byrne-Jones'*

The Brasses. Above and surrounding the Vestry door, you will see some of the finest brasses in the whole of Sussex. These date from the 1500s and show, in exquisite detail, the fashions and dress of those times.

Many people come to make brass rubbings of them. Above the Vestry door is the **'Bolney Brass':** Bartholomew Bolney, who died in 1476 and Eleanor his wife; he is wearing armour, she is in a long gown with fur collar and cuffs and a mitred head-dress. He was Lord of the Manor of West Firle and in 1472, his daughter and heiress, Agnes, married William Gage, the ancestor of the present Lord of the Manor, Viscount Gage.

This William Gage was a son of Sir John Gage, who had married Eleanor St Clere, a considerable heiress with lands in Sussex.

Eleanor and John lived at the Manor house, close to the Priory of Heighton St Clere, the site of which you can see in Firle Park between the stew ponds (the fish larder for the Priory and Firle Place) and Heighton Street. By this Bolney marriage the two manors were joined and the Gage family has held them ever since.

To the north side of the Vestry door is a brass of a bearded figure in armour. This is probably George Gage, who died in 1569. The accompanying Latin text is somewhat haunting: *'What of the body of life? They are but a flower, dust, a shadow that fleeth away.'*

On the south side of the Vestry door is Thomas Gage, brother of George, and his wife Elizabeth and the two kneeling figures of their daughters. The Latin inscription reads: *'Here lies Thomas Gage, gentleman and his wife, Elizabeth, departed A.D. 1590, who had one son and two daughters, upon whose souls may God have mercy.'*

There are two more brasses below the Chancel step as well as the brass effigies on two of the Gage Altar Tombs in the Vestry.

The Vestry (formerly The Chapel) houses three most impressive **Gage Altar Tombs**. One has recumbent alabaster effigies and heraldic brass; the others have brass effigies and shields.

They were all designed and executed by Garat Johnson. His original drawings for the design are preserved in Firle Place. The memorials were commissioned by John Gage in about 1595.

The recumbent effigies in alabaster are of Sir John Gage, K. G. (1556) and Philippa, his wife. Sir John is in armour, wearing a collar and garter of the Order of the Garter with the Gage crest, a ram, at his feet. Philippa, in a long gown has at her feet the Guldeford crest, a trunk of a tree in flames. Above the tomb there is a brass inscription in Latin, which is from Job, 19, verse 25 and reads: *'For I know that my redeemer liveth and that he shall stand at the latter day upon the earth.'*

A similar tomb placed against a recess in the north wall of the Vestry has brass effigies of St John's son, Sir Edward Gage, died 1569 and of Edward's wife Elizabeth. Their standing figures are turned towards one another, Sir Edward in armour and Elizabeth in a long gown with full sleeves, open to show her embroidered underdress.

Above the short inscription are two plates of arms. Sir Edward was the eldest son of Sir John. He was made Knight of the Bath at Queen Mary's accession to the throne. He was Sheriff of Surrey and Sussex. Elizabeth (Parker) was his first wife; he later married Joan, daughter of Sir Richard Sackville of Buckhurst. He had nine sons and five daughters.

The third tomb, set against a recess at the western end of the north wall of the Vestry is of John Gage, who died in 1595. John Gage was Sir John's grandson and it was he who commissioned these monuments to the family. His brass depicts himself and his two wives, Elizabeth (Littleton) and Margaret (Copley). Garat Johnson's drawing of these brasses has the criticisms of the client as well as the comments of the sculptor in the margin. The inscription and three shields are in the wall at the back of the monument.

Dominating the Vestry with its vibrant colours and sheer natural beauty is the **John Piper Window**, *'A Homage to William Blake's Book of Job'*, installed in 1985, in memory of The Rt. Hon. Henry Rainald, Sixth Viscount Gage, K. C. V. O., Who succeeded to the Viscountcy in his 17th year in 1912 and died on 27th of February 1982.

The window depicts the Tree of Life in the heavenly Jerusalem (Revelations 22:2). It was made by David Wasley with an inscription by John Skelton.

Lord Gage was a true pilgrim, dedicated to serving country, community and church, rooted in Firle yet caring for much beyond. He was greatly esteemed and is lovingly remembered.

The Chancel. Above the altar there is a **stained glass window** with its original stained glass, depicting The Crucifixion. **The Victorian wall tiles** are said to be by **William Morris**. The Chancel Arch is 14th century. The choir stalls date from 1904.

On the south wall, there is a **13th century Piscina**: when Firle Church was Roman Catholic, it was deemed that any remaining consecrated communion wine must be untouched by human hand and should be poured away into the Piscina from where it would descend straight into the earth. The Church of England requires the Vicar to consume any remaining communion wine.

Below the Chancel Step there are two more **17th-century Brasses.** The brass on the north side depicts the shrouded figure of Mary Howard, wife of Sir William Howard, a connection of the Duke of Norfolk, who died at Firle in 1638. The brass on the south side bears a charming inscription of Alice, wife of Thomas Levett, Vicar of Firle, 1676.

Note the restored **Clerestory windows** and the beautiful original cinquefoil in the East Gable of the Nave.

In the South Aisle is the **Lady Chapel.** On the south wall, there are memorials to both World Wars.

In the north wall of the Lady Chapel, within a narrow archway there is a blocked doorway leading by a spiral flight of stone stairs to the Rood Loft, 1501.

The Rood Loft was a small gallery high above the Chancel Steps. On the Rood loft was the main Cross in the Church. The priest and attendants would ascend to the Rood Loft in order to read out The Gospel to the congregation. The flight of stone stairs still exists, though invisible to us, but alas, the Rood Loft is no longer.

Behind the Altar of the Lady Chapel, the window still has its **Mediaeval 13th century stained glass**. Local worshippers took the glass and hid it for safekeeping at the time when Puritans were smashing up evidence of Catholicism. The glass was subsequently replaced but some of the pieces have been put back in the wrong places. Nonetheless, the colours remain very vibrant and are a great reminder of hope at that time.

All the pillars in the church are 13th century.

The churchyard.

In the lovely old **Churchyard**, just beyond the yew tree, by the north wall, you will find the graves of Vanessa Bell and Duncan Grant, stalwart members of the 'The Bloomsbury Group', who lived at Charleston Farmhouse, not far from Firle.

For a time, Virginia Woolf lived at Firle in The Street at Little Talland. The Bloomsbury Group painted the wonderful murals at nearby Berwick Church. Interestingly, Beddingham Church, sister church to Firle, was clearly once painted with murals and it is very likely that Firle Church was too, long ago.

Also in the graveyard, to the north of the church, you will see five graves of the Booker family. In their benevolence, they have left a bequest which pays for the upkeep of our graveyard.

Some History

The Prebendary of Firle has a stall at Chichester Cathedral and is under the patronage of the Bishop of Chichester and the Dean of Windsor.

The extant unbroken record of 60 vicars at Firle dates from 1197. In recent years notable lay preachers have been Lord Hailsham, then the Lord High Chancellor of all England, and the Earl of Longford, one of the senior peers of the realm.

At the time of the great tribulations when Roman Catholics and Protestants waged what they both believed was a moral and spiritual war for the true way of Christian thought and worship, Firle managed to hold the middle ground.

Its continued allegiance to the Roman form of mass was sustained by the Gage's even in times when Queen Elizabeth's supporters believed that many followers of papal mass had automatically supported Queen Mary and had had sympathies with Spain.

Fear was the mainspring of anxiety and this led to hatred and imprisonment for some, torture for others and persecution for many.

No wonder there was a backlash after Queen Mary's reign during which 16 Protestants were martyred by being burnt at the stake in Lewes between 1555-57. The High Sheriff of Lewes, Sir Edward Gage, had to attend those barbarous acts as indeed, previously Sir John Gage, Constable of the Tower, had attended the execution of Lady Jane Grey and the Dudleys. He was Lord Chamberlain of Queen Mary's household and appointed in charge of the young Princess Elizabeth.

As Protestantism swept the land, the church lost its holy water stoop at the south porch but in general the damage was very minor, the stained glass having been removed for safekeeping.

Many years later when it was restored some of the glass in the Lady Chapel was incorrectly reinserted and has been left as a witness to those days. What drama this Sanctuary has endured, from the destruction of the great Priory of St Pancreas at Lewes in 1537.

Anguish continued to brood over the land and in 1588 Firle Beacon was repaired to alert Sussex Yeomen to the dangers of the Spanish Armada.

So Firle church, a sanctuary of the Catholic and Apostolic church owing allegiance to Rome became after the Civil War, a Protestant reformed Church using the new Common prayer book in 1662.

Whilst the Gages were Catholic and Royalist only 2 miles away at Glynde there was the stronghold of Colonel Morley, a prominent puritan and Cromwellian leader.

That competition still today exists between the two villages and is now largely the subject of the cricket match, but through this historical vicissitudes the Parish Church of St Peter has remained a sanctuary of peace and beauty.

In the first Great War 1914-18 the blows were not physical to the land but spiritual to the Firle families, 11 young men lost their lives and many more were wounded or gassed.

In the second Great War, 1939 - 1945 Firle was more actively involved with the assault of the enemy air forces as numerous dogfights, a major part of the Battle of Britain, took place immediately overhead.

This battle must have been in the minds of Duncan Grant and Quentin Bell as they painted the frescos in Berwick church.

In the lovely panels on the altar rail are the four seasons in the Sussex countryside: Spring, Summer, Autumn and Winter, with the four seasons of life: birth, first Communion, marriage and death; but overhead against the blue sky and the faces of many people from Firle, the Downs and Firle Beacon, symbols of the eternity of life and of the pleasant land which surround St Peter's Church.

Sadness is seen amongst the loveliness, death amongst life and the trivia of the daily round.

As Firle Beacon stands out amidst the soft downland curves and a warning torch in time, so stands out Roman Conquest, Norman Invasion, the Battle of Lewes, Crecy, the Armada fleet, the Napoleonic threat, the first Great War, the world War, and so too does the Mount of Cavalry stand out above all time.

On Armada Sunday in July 1988, the priest in Firle, the Reverend Canon Woodward, quoted the Hugh Barnes-Yallowley poem:

Climb we the Ancient Downland ways
Where our Stone Age fathers trod
Seek in the rolling Sussex Downs
The highest greenways of God
Lift our eyes to the strong smooth hills
Encircling our homes and lives;
Here is peace and strength to our wills
And the love that never dies.

Sunrise, sunset, red,gold the sky
Raise over sacred Barrows.
A beacon of light from on high
The plough turning life's furrows
As it strikes on the flints of time;
We glimpse in Armada fires
A burning bush and Holy sign
The spark of the Light Divine.

Safe in the arms decreed by time
Black Cap Down to Caburn Mount
This village lies, a timeless sign
Of our loving God the fount
Of living waters flowing true
Life to sheep and golden grain
Springs from the well.

Now, thank the Lord God who made us
To dwell in this pleasant land
Raise thankful hearts for the blessings
Received from His generous hand
Climb we the ancient Downland way
Where our Stone Age fathers trod
Seek in the rolling Sussex Downs
The hidden greenways of God.

In this Sanctuary has trembled a spark breaking out as a star in Eternity, and in the timelessness the voice of Firle men say with the Psalmist voice of 3000 years ago *'The lot has fallen unto me in a fairground. Yes, I have a goodly heritage'.*

21151417R00026

Printed in Poland
by Amazon Fulfillment
Poland Sp. z o.o., Wrocław